MAD LIBS® FOR THE FANS

by Katie Fehrenbaker

CAITLIN CLARK EDITION

MAD LIBS
An imprint of Penguin Random House LLC
1745 Broadway, New York, New York 10019

First published in the United States of America by Mad Libs,
an imprint of Penguin Random House LLC, 2025

Mad Libs format and text copyright © 2025 by Penguin Random House LLC
Cover illustration copyright © 2025 by Jacqueline Li

Concept created by Roger Price & Leonard Stern

Cover illustration by Jacqueline Li

Photo credit: cover: (water bottle) Elena Chernykh/iStock/Getty Images

Penguin Random House values and supports copyright. Copyright fuels creativity,
encourages diverse voices, promotes free speech, and creates a vibrant culture. Thank you
for buying an authorized edition of this book and for complying with copyright laws by not
reproducing, scanning, or distributing any part of it in any form without permission. You are
supporting writers and allowing Penguin Random House to continue to publish books for
every reader. Please note that no part of this book may be used or reproduced in any
manner for the purpose of training artificial intelligence technologies or systems.

MAD LIBS and logo are registered trademarks of Penguin Random House LLC.

Visit us online at penguinrandomhouse.com.

Printed in the United States of America

ISBN 9798217050956
1 3 5 7 9 10 8 6 4 2
COMR

The authorized representative in the EU for product safety and compliance is
Penguin Random House Ireland, Morrison Chambers, 32 Nassau Street,
Dublin D02 YH68, Ireland, https://eu-contact.penguin.ie.

MAD LIBS®
INSTRUCTIONS

MAD LIBS® is a game for people who don't like games! It can be played by one, two, three, four, or forty.

• RIDICULOUSLY SIMPLE DIRECTIONS

In this tablet you will find stories containing blank spaces where words are left out. One player, the READER, selects one of these stories. The READER does not tell anyone what the story is about. Instead, he/she asks the other players, the WRITERS, to give him/her words. These words are used to fill in the blank spaces in the story.

• TO PLAY

The READER asks each WRITER in turn to call out a word—an adjective or a noun or whatever the space calls for—and uses them to fill in the blank spaces in the story. The result is a MAD LIBS® game.

When the READER then reads the completed MAD LIBS® game to the other players, they will discover that they have written a story that is fantastic, screamingly funny, shocking, silly, crazy, or just plain dumb—depending upon which words each WRITER called out.

• EXAMPLE (*Before* and *After*)

"_____!" he said _____
         EXCLAMATION   ADVERB

as he jumped into his convertible _____ and
                                           NOUN

drove off with his _____ wife.
                         ADJECTIVE

"_____OUCH_____!" he said ___HAPPILY___
         EXCLAMATION   ADVERB

as he jumped into his convertible ___CAT___ and
                                           NOUN

drove off with his ___BRAVE___ wife.
                         ADJECTIVE

MAD LIBS
QUICK REVIEW

In case you have forgotten what adjectives, adverbs, nouns, and verbs are, here is a quick review:

An ADJECTIVE describes something or somebody. *Lumpy, soft, ugly, messy,* and *short* are adjectives.

An ADVERB tells how something is done. It modifies a verb and usually ends in "ly." *Modestly, stupidly, greedily,* and *carefully* are adverbs.

A NOUN is the name of a person, place, or thing. *Sidewalk, umbrella, bridle, bathtub,* and *nose* are nouns.

A VERB is an action word. *Run, pitch, jump,* and *swim* are verbs. Put the verbs in past tense if the directions say PAST TENSE. *Ran, pitched, jumped,* and *swam* are verbs in the past tense.

When we ask for A PLACE, we mean any sort of place: a country or city (*Spain, Cleveland*) or a room (*bathroom, kitchen*).

An EXCLAMATION or SILLY WORD is any sort of funny sound, gasp, grunt, or outcry, like *Wow!, Ouch!, Whomp!, Ick!,* and *Gadzooks!*

When we ask for specific words, like a NUMBER, a COLOR, an ANIMAL, or a PART OF THE BODY, we mean a word that is one of those things, like *seven, blue, horse,* or *head*.

When we ask for a PLURAL, it means more than one. For example, *cat* pluralized is *cats*.

MAD LIBS® is fun to play with friends, but you can also play it by yourself! To begin with, DO NOT look at the story on the page below. Fill in the blanks on this page with the words called for. Then, using the words you have selected, fill in the blank spaces in the story.

Now you've created your own hilarious MAD LIBS® game!

EARLY MORNING PRACTICE

A SOUND _____

NOUN _____

NUMBER _____

ADJECTIVE _____

VERB (PAST TENSE) _____

PERSON YOU KNOW _____

VEHICLE _____

VERB _____

TYPE OF FOOD _____

TYPE OF BUILDING _____

CELEBRITY _____

NOUN _____

ANIMAL _____

TYPE OF LIQUID _____

COLOR _____

FIRST NAME _____

NOUN _____

ADJECTIVE _____

MAD LIBS

EARLY MORNING PRACTICE

_____! Ugh, there goes my alarm _____. How
   A SOUND   NOUN

is it _____ a.m. already? I'm feeling extra _____
     NUMBER   ADJECTIVE

this morning. Getting out of my bed is easier _____
                                              VERB (PAST TENSE)

than done. By the time I'm in my uniform, _____ has
                                         PERSON YOU KNOW

already started the _____ to take me to practice. I
                         VEHICLE

_____ a piece of _____ and head out the door.
  VERB   TYPE OF FOOD

On the drive to the _____, I can't help but wonder
                         TYPE OF BUILDING

where _____ finds the motivation. If I want to grow up
        CELEBRITY

and be the next G.O.A.T. basketball player, I've got to put a pep in

my _____ for early morning practices. At the gym, I'm
     NOUN

working so hard that I'm sweating like a/an _____.
                                             ANIMAL

_____ drenches my _____ pinny. When
TYPE OF LIQUID   COLOR

Coach _____ finally blows the _____ and
       FIRST NAME   NOUN

tells us to hit the showers, I feel _____ and ready for
                                  ADJECTIVE

the day ahead!

From MAD LIBS®: FOR THE FANS: CAITLIN CLARK EDITION • Copyright © 2025 by Penguin Random House LLC

MAD LIBS® is fun to play with friends, but you can also play it by yourself! To begin with, DO NOT look at the story on the page below. Fill in the blanks on this page with the words called for. Then, using the words you have selected, fill in the blank spaces in the story.

Now you've created your own hilarious MAD LIBS® game!

FAN MAIL

CELEBRITY _____

YOUR NAME _____

NUMBER _____

CITY _____

VERB ENDING IN "ING" _____

SOMETHING ALIVE _____

NOUN _____

OCCUPATION _____

VERB _____

PLURAL NOUN _____

NOUN _____

VERB ENDING IN "ING" _____

ADJECTIVE _____

TYPE OF FOOD _____

TYPE OF BUILDING _____

PERSON YOU KNOW _____

VERB _____

YOUR NAME _____

MAD LIBS®

FAN MAIL

Dear _____,
␣␣␣␣␣␣␣␣␣␣CELEBRITY

My name is _____ and I'm _____ years old. I live
␣␣␣␣␣␣␣␣␣␣␣␣␣␣␣YOUR NAME␣␣␣␣␣␣␣␣␣␣␣␣␣␣␣␣␣NUMBER

in the suburbs of _____ and love _____
␣␣␣␣␣␣␣␣␣␣␣␣␣␣␣␣␣␣␣␣␣CITY␣␣␣␣␣␣␣␣␣␣␣␣␣␣␣␣␣␣␣␣␣␣␣␣␣␣␣VERB ENDING IN "ING"

basketball and hanging out with my _____. I'm
␣␣␣SOMETHING ALIVE

writing you this _____ to let you know that you are my
␣␣␣␣␣␣␣␣␣␣␣␣␣␣␣␣␣␣NOUN

all-time favorite _____. When I watch your games on
␣␣␣␣␣␣␣␣␣␣␣␣␣␣␣␣␣OCCUPATION

television, I am inspired to _____ up and be just like you.
␣␣␣␣␣␣␣␣␣␣␣␣␣␣␣␣␣␣␣␣␣␣␣␣␣␣␣VERB

Do you have any advice on how to get better at _____?
␣␣␣PLURAL NOUN

I'm great at shooting foul shots, but my _____-handling
␣␣NOUN

skills could use some improvement. If you are _____
␣␣VERB ENDING IN "ING"

this, can you _____ please with a/an _____
␣␣␣␣␣␣␣␣␣␣␣␣␣␣␣ADJECTIVE␣␣␣␣␣␣␣␣␣␣␣␣␣␣␣␣␣␣␣␣␣␣␣␣␣TYPE OF FOOD

on top send me tickets to your game? It would change my life forever

and make me the coolest kid in the _____. I bet even
␣␣␣␣␣␣␣␣␣␣␣␣␣␣␣␣␣␣␣␣␣␣␣␣␣␣␣␣␣␣␣␣␣␣␣␣TYPE OF BUILDING

_____ would be jealous! I hope you _____
PERSON YOU KNOW␣␣␣␣␣␣␣␣␣␣␣␣␣␣␣␣␣␣␣␣␣␣␣␣␣␣␣␣␣␣␣␣␣␣VERB

me a letter back soon!

Your fan,

_____
␣␣␣YOUR NAME

From MAD LIBS®: FOR THE FANS: CAITLIN CLARK EDITION • Copyright © 2025 by Penguin Random House LLC

MAD LIBS® is fun to play with friends, but you can also play it by yourself! To begin with, DO NOT look at the story on the page below. Fill in the blanks on this page with the words called for. Then, using the words you have selected, fill in the blank spaces in the story.

Now you've created your own hilarious MAD LIBS® game!

THE HISTORY OF THE GAME

VERB _____

VERB (PAST TENSE) _____

ADJECTIVE _____

TYPE OF FOOD _____

NUMBER _____

OCCUPATION _____

SILLY WORD _____

ADJECTIVE _____

SOMETHING ALIVE (PLURAL) _____

ARTICLE OF CLOTHING (PLURAL) _____

NOUN _____

LETTER OF THE ALPHABET _____

VERB (PAST TENSE) _____

CELEBRITY _____

FIRST NAME _____

LAST NAME _____

NOUN _____

MAD LIBS

THE HISTORY OF THE GAME

The game of basketball's roots _____ back to 1891 when
                                    VERB
James Naismith founded the game. The rules _____
                                              VERB (PAST TENSE)
similar to those today with some _____ exceptions.
                                      ADJECTIVE
For example, they used _____ baskets instead of
                         TYPE OF FOOD
nets! Imagine sinking a/an _____ into one of those! The
                              NUMBER
first _____ to compete professionally did so in 1898.
        OCCUPATION
_____! Team names ranged from the Millville
  SILLY WORD
Glass Blowers to the _____ _____.
                          ADJECTIVE   SOMETHING ALIVE (PLURAL)
Team uniforms were often _____ made
                            ARTICLE OF CLOTHING (PLURAL)
from sheep wool! Talk about _____ madness! The
                                 NOUN
WNB-_____ was established nearly one hundred
      LETTER OF THE ALPHABET
years later, but _____ in popularity with the rise of
                   VERB (PAST TENSE)
_____. Most famous for the _____
  CELEBRITY   FIRST NAME
_____ Effect, this player is credited with changing the
  LAST NAME
_____ forever.
  NOUN

From MAD LIBS®: FOR THE FANS: CAITLIN CLARK EDITION • Copyright © 2025 by Penguin Random House LLC

MAD LIBS® is fun to play with friends, but you can also play it by yourself! To begin with, DO NOT look at the story on the page below. Fill in the blanks on this page with the words called for. Then, using the words you have selected, fill in the blank spaces in the story.

Now you've created your own hilarious MAD LIBS® game!

TRAINING SEASON

ADJECTIVE _____

CELEBRITY _____

SOMETHING ALIVE _____

NOUN _____

ADJECTIVE _____

OCCUPATION _____

TYPE OF FOOD _____

VERB _____

NOUN _____

ADVERB _____

ANIMAL _____

VERB ENDING IN "ING" _____

PART OF THE BODY _____

PLURAL NOUN _____

ADJECTIVE _____

NUMBER _____

VERB _____

MAD LIBS
TRAINING SEASON

If you want to be as _____ as _____, you have
                ADJECTIVE   CELEBRITY

to put in the work. As a wise _____ once said, "There
                                  SOMETHING ALIVE

is no _____ for _____ work." To be the best
       NOUN   ADJECTIVE

_____, here's what you need to do ahead of your first
OCCUPATION

game.

Step One: Fuel your body with _____ before you practice.
                                             TYPE OF FOOD

It's essential to _____ a balanced _____!
                 VERB   NOUN

Step Two: Stay _____ active throughout your day, whether
                    ADVERB

it's walking your _____, carrying your backpack, or
                       ANIMAL

_____ your chores.
VERB ENDING IN "ING"

Step Three: Be sure to take some time to rest your _____.
                                                           PART OF THE BODY

Soreness is to be expected, but stay clear of any sharp _____
                                                                     PLURAL NOUN

in the area.

Step Four: Lastly, be a/an _____ teammate to those
                                ADJECTIVE

around you and play as _____ on the court.
                            NUMBER

If you _____ these steps, you're destined to have an awesome
         VERB

season!

From MAD LIBS®: FOR THE FANS: CAITLIN CLARK EDITION • Copyright © 2025 by Penguin Random House LLC

MAD LIBS® is fun to play with friends, but you can also play it by yourself! To begin with, DO NOT look at the story on the page below. Fill in the blanks on this page with the words called for. Then, using the words you have selected, fill in the blank spaces in the story.

Now you've created your own hilarious MAD LIBS® game!

DRAFT DAY

SOMETHING ALIVE (PLURAL) _____

VERB (PAST TENSE) _____

NUMBER _____

TYPE OF BUILDING _____

COLOR _____

ARTICLE OF CLOTHING (PLURAL) _____

PLURAL NOUN _____

CELEBRITY _____

NUMBER _____

TYPE OF EVENT _____

VERB _____

OCCUPATION (PLURAL) _____

A SOUND (PLURAL) _____

VERB ENDING IN "ING" _____

ADVERB _____

VERB _____

MAD LIBS
DRAFT DAY

Ladies and _____ of the media,
           SOMETHING ALIVE (PLURAL)

You are hereby _____ to attend the 20-_____
                VERB (PAST TENSE)   NUMBER

Draft. It'll be held in the _____ at 7:30 in the evening.
                             TYPE OF BUILDING

The attire is _____ tie, although _____
                COLOR   ARTICLE OF CLOTHING (PLURAL)

are not required. Please read the following _____
                                              PLURAL NOUN

carefully: Like you, we anticipate that _____ will be
                                          CELEBRITY

drafted as the number _____ overall pick in the first round.
                       NUMBER

However, nothing is official until this year's _____.
                                                 TYPE OF EVENT

We _____ attendees to not create any disruptions when
      VERB

this person is chosen, and those who do will be removed by the

_____. Disruptions include, but are not limited to,
OCCUPATION (PLURAL)

cheers, _____, or whistles. _____
         A SOUND (PLURAL)   VERB ENDING IN "ING"

is permitted. We will uphold this policy to ensure the event runs

_____ for all in attendance.
   ADVERB

We _____ forward to welcoming you.
      VERB

From MAD LIBS®: FOR THE FANS: CAITLIN CLARK EDITION • Copyright © 2025 by Penguin Random House LLC

MAD LIBS® is fun to play with friends, but you can also play it by yourself! To begin with, DO NOT look at the story on the page below. Fill in the blanks on this page with the words called for. Then, using the words you have selected, fill in the blank spaces in the story.

Now you've created your own hilarious MAD LIBS® game!

A GAME OF PICKUP

VERB _____

NOUN _____

SOMETHING ALIVE _____

VERB _____

VERB _____

PLURAL NOUN _____

A PLACE _____

EXCLAMATON _____

NOUN _____

SOMETHING ALIVE (PLURAL) _____

ADJECTIVE _____

PLURAL NOUN _____

ADVERB _____

PERSON YOU KNOW _____

NOUN _____

MAD LIBS®
A GAME OF PICKUP

Person 1: Hey, want to _____ some hoops with us?
　　　　　　　　　　　　　　　VERB

Person 2: I love _____ , but I'm not sure I should be talking
　　　　　　　　　　　NOUN
to you. My _____ said to never _____
　　　　　　　SOMETHING ALIVE　　　　　　　　　　　　　　VERB
to strangers.

Person 1: It's _____-up basketball! We're all _____!
　　　　　　　　　　VERB　　　　　　　　　　　　　　　　　PLURAL NOUN
C'mon and join us on (the) _____ .
　　　　　　　　　　　　　　　A PLACE

Person 2: _____! Pickup sounds like a/an _____
　　　　　　　EXCLAMATION　　　　　　　　　　　　　　　　　　NOUN
of fun and a great way to meet new _____ .
　　　　　　　　　　　　　　　　　　　SOMETHING ALIVE (PLURAL)

Person 1: Even more _____ , you'll learn some new
　　　　　　　　　　　　　　ADJECTIVE
_____ from your pickup team!
PLURAL NOUN

Person 2: I can _____ wait to tell _____ about
　　　　　　　　　　　　ADVERB　　　　　　　　　PERSON YOU KNOW
this! Can I be _____ guard?
　　　　　　　　　　NOUN

From MAD LIBS®: FOR THE FANS: CAITLIN CLARK EDITION • Copyright © 2025 by Penguin Random House LLC

MAD LIBS® is fun to play with friends, but you can also play it by yourself! To begin with, DO NOT look at the story on the page below. Fill in the blanks on this page with the words called for. Then, using the words you have selected, fill in the blank spaces in the story.

Now you've created your own hilarious MAD LIBS® game!

MAKING A
LASTING IMPRESSION

SOMETHING ALIVE (PLURAL) _____

ADJECTIVE _____

NUMBER _____

YOUR NAME _____

ADJECTIVE _____

NOUN _____

ADJECTIVE _____

A PLACE _____

OCCUPATION (PLURAL) _____

NOUN _____

VERB ENDING IN "ING" _____

PLURAL NOUN _____

ADVERB _____

VERB _____

OCCUPATION _____

MAD LIBS
MAKING A LASTING IMPRESSION

Want to change the history of sports for _____
                                          SOMETHING ALIVE (PLURAL)
forever? Follow these _____ steps to create the _____
                         ADJECTIVE   NUMBER
and only "_____ Effect."
           YOUR NAME

Step One: Find what makes you _____ and stand out
                                      ADJECTIVE
from the _____.
            NOUN

Step Two: Practice your _____ skill until you are better
                               ADJECTIVE
at it than everyone in (the) _____.
                                A PLACE

Step Three: Inspire budding _____ to discover what
                                  OCCUPATION (PLURAL)
makes them unique. They are the future of the _____.
                                                    NOUN

Step Four: Welcome in new fans by _____ people to
                                         VERB ENDING IN "ING"
watch your _____.
               PLURAL NOUN

Step Five: _____, don't forget to _____ the
                  ADVERB   VERB
people who helped you get to where you are today! You are a huge
role _____ to them!
       OCCUPATION

From MAD LIBS®: FOR THE FANS: CAITLIN CLARK EDITION • Copyright © 2025 by Penguin Random House LLC

MAD LIBS® is fun to play with friends, but you can also play it by yourself! To begin with, DO NOT look at the story on the page below. Fill in the blanks on this page with the words called for. Then, using the words you have selected, fill in the blank spaces in the story.

Now you've created your own hilarious MAD LIBS® game!

WHAT KIND OF TEAMMATE ARE YOU?

VERB _____

VERB _____

TYPE OF CONTAINER _____

PLURAL NOUN _____

VERB ENDING IN "S" _____

ADJECTIVE _____

A SOUND _____

ADJECTIVE _____

TYPE OF FOOD _____

NUMBER _____

LETTER OF THE ALPHABET _____

ADJECTIVE _____

ADJECTIVE _____

CITY _____

PLURAL NOUN _____

PART OF THE BODY (PLURAL) _____

ADJECTIVE _____

MAD LIBS
WHAT KIND OF TEAMMATE ARE YOU?

1. What do you _____ about yourself? (a) how you
   VERB

   _____ those around you, (b) your _____-
   VERB   TYPE OF CONTAINER

   half-full optimism, (c) your ability to make sure _____
                                                      PLURAL NOUN

   get along

2. What best _____ your personality? (a) a/an
              VERB ENDING IN "S"

   _____ lion, hear you _____! (b) a/an
   ADJECTIVE   A SOUND

   _____ puppy, (c) a/an _____ bee
   ADJECTIVE   TYPE OF FOOD

3. What do you want to be when you turn _____ years
                                         NUMBER

   old? (a) President of the US-_____, (b) a teacher
                                 LETTER OF THE ALPHABET

   who makes homework _____! (c) a chef in the
                      ADJECTIVE

   most _____ restaurant in _____!
        ADJECTIVE   CITY

Answers:

If you got mostly *a*'s, you're a leader, connecting _____
                                                     PLURAL NOUN

to work together. If you got mostly *b*'s, you're a cheerleader with

pom-poms in your _____! If you got mostly *c*'s,
                 PART OF THE BODY (PLURAL)

you're the _____ team player!
           ADJECTIVE

From MAD LIBS®: FOR THE FANS: CAITLIN CLARK EDITION • Copyright © 2025 by Penguin Random House LLC

MAD LIBS® is fun to play with friends, but you can also play it by yourself! To begin with, DO NOT look at the story on the page below. Fill in the blanks on this page with the words called for. Then, using the words you have selected, fill in the blank spaces in the story.

Now you've created your own hilarious MAD LIBS® game!

AN INTERVIEW WITH C.C.

SOMETHING ALIVE _____

CELEBRITY _____

VERB ENDING IN "ING" _____

VERB _____

NOUN _____

ADVERB _____

PLURAL NOUN _____

ADJECTIVE _____

NOUN _____

CITY _____

TYPE OF LIQUID _____

OCCUPATION _____

PLURAL NOUN _____

VERB _____

PART OF THE BODY _____

MAD LIBS

AN INTERVIEW WITH C.C.

Interviewer: Please welcome the _____, the myth, the
                                    SOMETHING ALIVE

legend, _____!
         CELEBRITY

C.C.: Thank you for _____ me!
                        VERB ENDING IN "ING"

Interviewer: Let's _____ right in! Have you been enjoying
                        VERB

your rookie _____?
             NOUN

C.C.: _____, without a doubt! I'm learning so much each
          ADVERB

day from my _____ and coaches.
             PLURAL NOUN

Interviewer: What's been the most _____ challenge adjusting
                                       ADJECTIVE

to life in the _____?
                NOUN

C.C.: Hmmm, although _____ is a great place to play,
                          CITY

it's hard to grab a cup of _____ without stopping for
                            TYPE OF LIQUID

a selfie! Life as a professional _____ is new, but the
                                  OCCUPATION

_____ are amazing.
PLURAL NOUN

Interviewer: What is a piece of advice you'd like to _____
                                                          VERB

young fans watching?

C.C.: Keep your _____ in the game and don't give up!
                    PART OF THE BODY

From MAD LIBS®: FOR THE FANS: CAITLIN CLARK EDITION • Copyright © 2025 by Penguin Random House LLC

MAD LIBS® is fun to play with friends, but you can also play it by yourself! To begin with, DO NOT look at the story on the page below. Fill in the blanks on this page with the words called for. Then, using the words you have selected, fill in the blank spaces in the story.

Now you've created your own hilarious MAD LIBS® game!

A NEW RECORD

SOMETHING ALIVE (PLURAL) _____

CELEBRITY _____

PLURAL NOUN _____

NUMBER _____

PERSON YOU KNOW _____

LAST NAME _____

VERB _____

NOUN _____

VERB (PAST TENSE) _____

TYPE OF BUILDING _____

SAME LAST NAME _____

ADVERB _____

VERB _____

ADJECTIVE _____

NUMBER _____

NOUN _____

OCCUPATION _____

PLURAL NOUN _____

MAD LIBS
A NEW RECORD

Sports for _____ will never be the same. _____
           SOMETHING ALIVE (PLURAL)   CELEBRITY
broke the WNBA record for most _____ scored in a game,
                                PLURAL NOUN
with a whopping _____. The record had previously been held
                  NUMBER
by _____, who claimed the title for several decades.
    PERSON YOU KNOW
_____ was projected to _____ the record by the
  LAST NAME   VERB
end of this year's regular _____, but surprised the world by
                              NOUN
doing so sooner. As you _____ moments ago, everyone
                           VERB (PAST TENSE)
in the _____ is overjoyed for _____.
       TYPE OF BUILDING   SAME LAST NAME
Play was paused _____ as teammates flooded the court
                    ADVERB
to _____ the rookie superstar. This moment represents
      VERB
_____ change for the future of the sport, as viewership
  ADJECTIVE
continues to rise by _____ percent each game. I believe it is just
                       NUMBER
the _____ for this _____, and there will
      NOUN   OCCUPATION
be many more broken _____ to come.
                       PLURAL NOUN

From MAD LIBS®: FOR THE FANS: CAITLIN CLARK EDITION • Copyright © 2025 by Penguin Random House LLC

MAD LIBS® is fun to play with friends, but you can also play it by yourself! To begin with, DO NOT look at the story on the page below. Fill in the blanks on this page with the words called for. Then, using the words you have selected, fill in the blank spaces in the story.

Now you've created your own hilarious MAD LIBS® game!

WHAT'S YOUR BEST HOOPS SKILL?

ADJECTIVE _____

ADJECTIVE _____

COUNTRY _____

ANIMAL (PLURAL) _____

ADJECTIVE _____

ADJECTIVE _____

TYPE OF FOOD _____

VERB _____

VERB (PAST TENSE) _____

NOUN _____

PERSON YOU KNOW _____

VERB ENDING IN "ING" _____

NOUN _____

PART OF THE BODY _____

VERB _____

A PLACE _____

NOUN _____

VERB _____

MAD LIBS
WHAT'S YOUR BEST HOOPS SKILL?

1. What is your _____ vacation spot? (a) a/an _____
   ADJECTIVE   ADJECTIVE
   beach, (b) a faraway city in _____ , (c) in the countryside
                                 COUNTRY
   alongside _____
              ANIMAL (PLURAL)

2. What's your go-to _____ treat? (a) a/an _____
                      ADJECTIVE   ADJECTIVE
   fudge sundae, (b) a bowl of fresh _____ , (c)
                                       TYPE OF FOOD
   _____ -corn with butter
      VERB

3. What would you do if you _____ the lottery? (a)
                              VERB (PAST TENSE)
   donate it all to a/an _____ , (b) buy _____
                            NOUN   PERSON YOU KNOW
   a car, (c) take yourself _____
                              VERB ENDING IN "ING"

Answers:

If you got mostly *a*'s, you're an All- _____ at Behind the
                                          NOUN
_____ . Nobody can _____ the ball from you!
 PART OF THE BODY   VERB
If you got mostly *b*'s, your best move is (the) _____ -oop.
                                                    A PLACE
Your _____ never sees it coming! If you got mostly *c*'s,
        NOUN
you set the greatest _____ -and-roll that the game's ever
                         VERB
witnessed.

From MAD LIBS®: FOR THE FANS: CAITLIN CLARK EDITION • Copyright © 2025 by Penguin Random House LLC

MAD LIBS® is fun to play with friends, but you can also play it by yourself! To begin with, DO NOT look at the story on the page below. Fill in the blanks on this page with the words called for. Then, using the words you have selected, fill in the blank spaces in the story.

Now you've created your own hilarious MAD LIBS® game!

PRE-GAME JITTERS SMOOTHIE

ADJECTIVE _____

NOUN _____

TYPE OF LIQUID _____

VERB _____

SOMETHING ALIVE _____

TYPE OF LIQUID _____

NUMBER _____

TYPE OF FOOD _____

TYPE OF LIQUID _____

ANIMAL _____

TYPE OF CONTAINER _____

LETTER OF THE ALPHABET _____

NUMBER _____

VERB ENDING IN "S" _____

ADJECTIVE _____

MAD LIBS
PRE-GAME JITTERS SMOOTHIE

Whenever I feel _____ before a game, I make myself a
           ADJECTIVE
pre- _____ smoothie. It's not just any _____. It has
       NOUN   TYPE OF LIQUID
powers to _____ even the most nervous _____.
            VERB   SOMETHING ALIVE
You will need:

- One _____-spoon of sugar
       TYPE OF LIQUID
- _____ scoops of protein powder
    NUMBER
- Half of a/an _____
                TYPE OF FOOD
- A cup of _____ from a/an _____
            TYPE OF LIQUID   ANIMAL

Combine and pour all of your ingredients into a/an _____.
                                                    TYPE OF CONTAINER
Blend it for as long as it takes to sing your _____-BCs
                                               LETTER OF THE ALPHABET
twice. Please enjoy at least _____ minutes before your game
                              NUMBER
_____ to ensure _____ results.
VERB ENDING IN "S"   ADJECTIVE

From MAD LIBS®: FOR THE FANS: CAITLIN CLARK EDITION • Copyright © 2025 by Penguin Random House LLC

MAD LIBS® is fun to play with friends, but you can also play it by yourself! To begin with, DO NOT look at the story on the page below. Fill in the blanks on this page with the words called for. Then, using the words you have selected, fill in the blank spaces in the story.

Now you've created your own hilarious MAD LIBS® game!

AN ODE TO BASKETBALL

VERB _____

ADJECTIVE _____

TYPE OF LIQUID _____

NUMBER _____

TYPE OF CONTAINER _____

A PLACE _____

PART OF THE BODY (PLURAL) _____

VERB _____

COLOR _____

ADJECTIVE _____

OCCUPATION _____

PLURAL NOUN _____

ADJECTIVE _____

A PLACE _____

MAD LIBS®

AN ODE TO BASKETBALL

Dribble, bounce, _____, and shoot—
                         VERB

being an all-star is not always _____.
                                        ADJECTIVE

As _____ drenches my brow,
        TYPE OF LIQUID

I net a/an _____, and the crowd cheers, "Wow!"
          NUMBER

_____-ball is the best.
TYPE OF CONTAINER

I'll put my _____ shot to the test.
             A PLACE

Through the _____ or around the back,
     PART OF THE BODY (PLURAL)

my opponents know I'm on the right _____.
                                                VERB

All I need is the _____ sphere and a net
               COLOR

to practice my _____ throws and be the best yet.
       ADJECTIVE

Point _____ or center,
  OCCUPATION

my skills make my _____ surrender.
      PLURAL NOUN

One day I'll be as _____ as Clark,
     ADJECTIVE

but until then, it's pickup in (the) _____!
        A PLACE

From MAD LIBS®: FOR THE FANS: CAITLIN CLARK EDITION • Copyright © 2025 by Penguin Random House LLC

MAD LIBS® is fun to play with friends, but you can also play it by yourself! To begin with, DO NOT look at the story on the page below. Fill in the blanks on this page with the words called for. Then, using the words you have selected, fill in the blank spaces in the story.

Now you've created your own hilarious MAD LIBS® game!

TRYING TIMES

COLOR _____

ANIMAL (PLURAL) _____

NOUN _____

NUMBER _____

VERB _____

ADJECTIVE _____

VERB ENDING IN "ING" _____

SOMETHING ALIVE _____

PERSON YOU KNOW _____

ADVERB _____

CELEBRITY _____

PART OF THE BODY _____

NOUN _____

OCCUPATION _____

LAST NAME _____

VERB ENDING IN "ING" _____

A PLACE _____

LETTER OF THE ALPHABET _____

MAD LIBS
TRYING TIMES

Dear Diary,

The basketball tryouts for my school's team, the _____
                                                        COLOR

_____, are today. It's been my _____ to
ANIMAL (PLURAL)   NOUN

make varsity since I was _____ years old. I could barely
                              NUMBER

even _____ a ball yet! Now that I'm older and more
          VERB

_____, I think I'm ready to make the team. I've been
ADJECTIVE

_____ with my _____ all summer,
VERB ENDING IN "ING"   SOMETHING ALIVE

and they think I show real potential. Sure, _____ is
                                                  PERSON YOU KNOW

_____ the best in the whole school, but there are still
ADVERB

plenty of spots for rookies like me. Just look at what _____
                                                             CELEBRITY

did during their rookie season! They broke the shooting record with

a broken _____. There's got to be _____
          PART OF THE BODY   NOUN

for me. _____ _____ said showing up
         OCCUPATION   LAST NAME

on time is _____ late, so I better run. Wish me luck
             VERB ENDING IN "ING"

out on (the) _____!
              A PLACE

XOX- _____,
      LETTER OF THE ALPHABET

Me

From MAD LIBS®: FOR THE FANS: CAITLIN CLARK EDITION • Copyright © 2025 by Penguin Random House LLC

MAD LIBS® is fun to play with friends, but you can also play it by yourself! To begin with, DO NOT look at the story on the page below. Fill in the blanks on this page with the words called for. Then, using the words you have selected, fill in the blank spaces in the story.

Now you've created your own hilarious MAD LIBS® game!

HOW TO SHOOT A THREE

VERB _____

NUMBER _____

ADJECTIVE _____

PART OF THE BODY (PLURAL) _____

VERB _____

ANIMAL _____

PLURAL NOUN _____

VERB ENDING IN "ING" _____

VERB _____

NOUN _____

PERSON YOU KNOW _____

PART OF THE BODY (PLURAL) _____

NOUN _____

A SOUND _____

NOUN _____

MAD LIBS®
HOW TO SHOOT A THREE

Struggling to _____ a/an _____-pointer? Look no
               VERB   NUMBER

further than this _____ guide!
                  ADJECTIVE

Step One: Keep a soft bend in your _____. It's
                                               PART OF THE BODY (PLURAL)

important to stay loose and _____ out the jitters.
                                 VERB

Step Two: Make a/an _____ sound to signal to your
                          ANIMAL

_____ that you're going to shoot the ball. This step is
PLURAL NOUN

also great for _____ the opponent.
              VERB ENDING IN "ING"

Step Three: When you _____, visualize the ball creating
                           VERB

a/an _____-like shape through the air. Don't forget to
        NOUN

strike a pose for _____ out in the crowd!
                PERSON YOU KNOW

Step Four: Close your _____ and make a/an
                             PART OF THE BODY (PLURAL)

_____ that it goes in.
NOUN

Step Five: Repeat steps one through four until . . . _____!
                                                             A SOUND

Game over, and your _____ won!
                      NOUN

From MAD LIBS®: FOR THE FANS: CAITLIN CLARK EDITION • Copyright © 2025 by Penguin Random House LLC

MAD LIBS® is fun to play with friends, but you can also play it by yourself! To begin with, DO NOT look at the story on the page below. Fill in the blanks on this page with the words called for. Then, using the words you have selected, fill in the blank spaces in the story.

Now you've created your own hilarious MAD LIBS® game!

THE TROPHIES TAKE A TUMBLE

A SOUND _____

EXCLAMATION _____

SOMETHING ALIVE _____

VERB _____

NOUN _____

PERSON YOU KNOW _____

VERB ENDING IN "ING" _____

TYPE OF BUILDING _____

PART OF THE BODY (PLURAL) _____

ADVERB _____

NUMBER _____

VERB (PAST TENSE) _____

LETTER OF THE ALPHABET _____

TYPE OF BUILDING _____

NOUN _____

NOUN _____

VERB _____

PERSON YOU KNOW _____

MAD LIBS®
THE TROPHIES TAKE A TUMBLE

Crash, clank, _____! _____! My
             A SOUND   EXCLAMATION
_____ is going to _____ me. How am I
SOMETHING ALIVE   VERB
supposed to clean up this _____ before _____ gets
                              NOUN   PERSON YOU KNOW
home?! Gosh, I know that I'm not supposed to be _____
                                                 VERB ENDING IN "ING"
my crossovers in the _____, but I was being careful.
                      TYPE OF BUILDING
The ball slipped out of my _____! It rolled
                            PART OF THE BODY (PLURAL)
_____, so I really have no idea how it shattered all _____
   ADVERB   NUMBER
trophies on the shelf. Do you think I'll be _____?
                                             VERB (PAST TENSE)
OM-_____. I can't miss the _____
    LETTER OF THE ALPHABET   TYPE OF BUILDING
dance on Saturday. That would be super unfair since I don't think
this _____ is my fault. The manufacturing _____
      NOUN   NOUN
should use better glue for their trophies! Well, time to _____
                                                          VERB
this mess before _____ gets home!
                  PERSON YOU KNOW

From MAD LIBS®: FOR THE FANS: CAITLIN CLARK EDITION • Copyright © 2025 by Penguin Random House LLC

MAD LIBS® is fun to play with friends, but you can also play it by yourself! To begin with, DO NOT look at the story on the page below. Fill in the blanks on this page with the words called for. Then, using the words you have selected, fill in the blank spaces in the story.

Now you've created your own hilarious MAD LIBS® game!

LOCKER ROOM TROUBLES

NOUN _____

PERSON YOU KNOW _____

VERB ENDING IN "ING" _____

LETTER OF THE ALPHABET _____

ANIMAL _____

NOUN _____

VERB _____

ADVERB _____

YOUR NAME _____

TYPE OF CONTAINER _____

NUMBER _____

OCCUPATION _____

ADJECTIVE _____

ARTICLE OF CLOTHING _____

NOUN _____

MAD LIBS®
LOCKER ROOM TROUBLES

Person 1: What in the _____ is that smell? _____,
             NOUN   PERSON YOU KNOW

are you _____ this?!
         VERB ENDING IN "ING"

Person 2: P-_____. You weren't kidding! Did a/an
                LETTER OF THE ALPHABET

_____ die in here or something?
   ANIMAL

Person 1: Beats me, but whatever it is sure seems like some toxic

_____. Wait, _____ here, I think found the source!
   NOUN   VERB

Person 2: You're _____ right! It's coming from _____'s
                      ADVERB   YOUR NAME

locker! Do you know their _____ combination?
                           TYPE OF CONTAINER

Person 1: Try _____, but we better call the _____ to
                   NUMBER   OCCUPATION

clean this out stat!

Person 2: I can't believe our star player left their _____
                                                          ADJECTIVE

_____ in here all _____!
ARTICLE OF CLOTHING   NOUN

From MAD LIBS®: FOR THE FANS: CAITLIN CLARK EDITION • Copyright © 2025 by Penguin Random House LLC

MAD LIBS® is fun to play with friends, but you can also play it by yourself! To begin with, DO NOT look at the story on the page below. Fill in the blanks on this page with the words called for. Then, using the words you have selected, fill in the blank spaces in the story.

Now you've created your own hilarious MAD LIBS® game!

CHILLING COURTSIDE

PERSON YOU KNOW _____

ADVERB _____

CELEBRITY _____

ADJECTIVE _____

PART OF THE BODY _____

TYPE OF LIQUID _____

ADJECTIVE _____

NUMBER _____

LAST NAME _____

FIRST NAME _____

OCCUPATION _____

SILLY WORD _____

CELEBRITY _____

PART OF THE BODY _____

A PLACE _____

VERB (PAST TENSE) _____

NOUN _____

MAD LIBS

CHILLING COURTSIDE

Last night, _____ and I sat courtside at a professional
                    PERSON YOU KNOW

basketball game. It was _____ magical to see _____
                              ADVERB   CELEBRITY

play live. They are even taller in person and so _____.
                                                       ADJECTIVE

Our seats were so close to the action that my _____
                                                  PART OF THE BODY

is sore from turning side to side. We could even smell the players'

_____. The game was so _____ that
   TYPE OF LIQUID   ADJECTIVE

we jumped out of our seats at least _____ times. Then,
                                          NUMBER

_____ fouled out in the fourth quarter, and Coach
     LAST NAME

_____ was thrown out after calling the _____
    FIRST NAME   OCCUPATION

a/an _____. Like they always do, _____
         SILLY WORD   CELEBRITY

played their _____ out and secured a/an _____
             PART OF THE BODY   A PLACE

team victory. At the buzzer, confetti _____ down, and
                                         VERB (PAST TENSE)

I got an autograph. It was the best _____ of my life!
                                          NOUN

From MAD LIBS®: FOR THE FANS: CAITLIN CLARK EDITION • Copyright © 2025 by Penguin Random House LLC

MAD LIBS® is fun to play with friends, but you can also play it by yourself! To begin with, DO NOT look at the story on the page below. Fill in the blanks on this page with the words called for. Then, using the words you have selected, fill in the blank spaces in the story.

Now you've created your own hilarious MAD LIBS® game!

LAUNDRY DAY

NOUN _____

ADJECTIVE _____

SOMETHING ALIVE _____

PLURAL NOUN _____

VERB ENDING IN "ING" _____

VERB _____

TYPE OF CONTAINER _____

ARTICLE OF CLOTHING (PLURAL) _____

NUMBER _____

CELEBRITY _____

VERB _____

SILLY WORD _____

ADJECTIVE _____

NOUN _____

PERSON YOU KNOW _____

NOUN _____

ADVERB _____

VERB _____

MAD LIBS
LAUNDRY DAY

Daily chores don't have to be a/an _____! They
                                        NOUN
can be a/an _____ way to practice your skills. Take it
               ADJECTIVE
from _____. I always used to dread my morning
        SOMETHING ALIVE
_____, but ever since I started _____ during
 PLURAL NOUN   VERB ENDING IN "ING"
that time, they seem to _____ by! Practice begins
                               VERB
with opening the _____, which will serve as your
                   TYPE OF CONTAINER
net. Now, bunch up your _____ into a compact
                         ARTICLE OF CLOTHING (PLURAL)
sphere. Take _____ steps away from the washing machine. If
              NUMBER
you want to try and shoot like _____, take a few more.
                                  CELEBRITY
_____ away! Before you can say _____, all
   VERB   SILLY WORD
of your _____ clothes will be in the _____, ready
         ADJECTIVE   NOUN
to be cleaned. Make sure _____ does not see you
                            PERSON YOU KNOW
having too much _____ doing the laundry. If they see
                     NOUN
you finished too _____, they'll become suspicious and
                    ADVERB
_____ you more chores!
    VERB

From MAD LIBS®: FOR THE FANS: CAITLIN CLARK EDITION • Copyright © 2025 by Penguin Random House LLC

MAD LIBS® is fun to play with friends, but you can also play it by yourself! To begin with, DO NOT look at the story on the page below. Fill in the blanks on this page with the words called for. Then, using the words you have selected, fill in the blank spaces in the story.

Now you've created your own hilarious MAD LIBS® game!

COMMERCIAL BREAK

CELEBRITY _____

ADVERB _____

NOUN _____

ADJECTIVE _____

TYPE OF LIQUID _____

PLURAL NOUN _____

ADJECTIVE _____

A PLACE _____

NOUN _____

COLOR _____

ANIMAL _____

PLURAL NOUN _____

VERB _____

TYPE OF LIQUID _____

NOUN _____

PART OF THE BODY _____

OCCUPATION _____

NUMBER _____

MAD LIBS

COMMERCIAL BREAK

The camera cuts to _____ practicing their dribbling
                        CELEBRITY

skills, _____ stopping when the whistle blows. They pivot
          ADVERB

to face the camera, grab a bottle of the _____, and say:
                                            NOUN

"When practice is _____, there's only one _____
                    ADJECTIVE   TYPE OF LIQUID

to replenish my energy. Packed with lots of electrolytes, vitamins, and

_____, it's the _____ boost to get me through
  PLURAL NOUN   ADJECTIVE

training on and off (the) _____.
                            A PLACE

Where there's a/an _____, there's _____
                      NOUN   COLOR

_____-ade. Let your _____ _____."
  ANIMAL   PLURAL NOUN   VERB

Disclaimer: This _____ may cause intense _____
                   TYPE OF LIQUID   NOUN

in the _____. If symptoms persist, please visit your
          PART OF THE BODY

_____ in the next _____ seconds.
  OCCUPATION   NUMBER

From MAD LIBS®: FOR THE FANS: CAITLIN CLARK EDITION • Copyright © 2025 by Penguin Random House LLC

MAD LIBS® is fun to play with friends, but you can also play it by yourself! To begin with, DO NOT look at the story on the page below. Fill in the blanks on this page with the words called for. Then, using the words you have selected, fill in the blank spaces in the story.

Now you've created your own hilarious MAD LIBS® game!

JUMBOTRON DISASTER

NOUN _____

NUMBER _____

ADJECTIVE _____

PERSON YOU KNOW _____

ADJECTIVE _____

ADVERB _____

PLURAL NOUN _____

SILLY WORD _____

PART OF THE BODY (PLURAL) _____

OCCUPATION _____

TYPE OF FOOD _____

VERB (PAST TENSE) _____

LAST NAME _____

VERB ENDING IN "ING" _____

ARTICLE OF CLOTHING _____

ADJECTIVE _____

CELEBRITY _____

NOUN _____

MAD LIBS

JUMBOTRON DISASTER

All my life, I've wanted to go to a live basket- _____ game.
                                                      NOUN
It's been my dream to have my _____ seconds of fame on the
                                   NUMBER
_____ screen. When _____ got me tickets to
   ADJECTIVE   PERSON YOU KNOW
see a C.C. game, I was _____! _____, all my
                             ADJECTIVE   ADVERB
_____ were about to come true! Or so I thought . . .
 PLURAL NOUN
When we arrived to _____ Center, I was so excited that
                          SILLY WORD
my _____ were shaking as I handed my ticket to
    PART OF THE BODY (PLURAL)
the _____. As soon as we got inside, we got _____
      OCCUPATION   TYPE OF FOOD
with extra toppings, my favorite! Moments later, the music started,
and the players _____ on the court. Upon seeing
                      VERB (PAST TENSE)
_____, I was so pumped that I jumped out of my seat,
   LAST NAME
with my food _____ all over my _____.
                 VERB ENDING IN "ING"   ARTICLE OF CLOTHING
To top it off, everyone saw it on the _____-tron, even
                                              ADJECTIVE
_____! At least I got my moment of _____!
  CELEBRITY   NOUN

From MAD LIBS®: FOR THE FANS: CAITLIN CLARK EDITION • Copyright © 2025 by Penguin Random House LLC

Download Mad Libs today!

Join the millions of Mad Libs fans creating wacky and wonderful stories on our apps!